RHINOCEROS BEETLE

By Catherine C. Finan

Consultant: Darin Collins, DVM
Director, Animal Health Programs, Woodland Park Zoo

BEARPORT
PUBLISHING

Minneapolis, Minnesota

Credits

cover, © Mark Brandon/Shutterstock and © Gun/Shutterstock; 3, © enterphoto/Shutterstock; 4, 5, © 92/1 Moo3 Huai Yang Kham Chun Phayao, Thailand 56150/iStock; 7, © Mark Brandon/Shutterstock; 8, © Lightboxx/ Shutterstock; 9, © Bonita R. Cheshier/Shutterstock; 11, © iaobzjls/iStock; 13, © imageBROKER/Alamy Stock Photo; 14, © LilKar/Shutterstock; 15, © Toa55/Shutterstock; 16, © kamnuan/Shutterstock; 17, © Lepidlizard/Wikipedia; 18, 19, © Mark Brandon/Shutterstock; 21, © wonderisland/Shutterstock; 23, © aodaodaodaod/Shutterstock

President: Jen Jenson
Director of Product Development: Spencer Brinker
Editor: Allison Juda
Designer: Micah Edel

Library of Congress Cataloging-in-Publication Data

Names: Finan, Catherine C., 1972 author.
Title: Rhinoceros beetle / Catherine C. Finan.
Description: Minneapolis, Minnesota : Bearport Publishing Company, [2021] |
  Series: Library of awesome animals | Includes bibliographical references and index.
Identifiers: LCCN 2020008973 (print) | LCCN 2020008974 (ebook) |
  ISBN 9781647471446 (library binding) | ISBN 9781647471552 (paperback) |
  ISBN 9781647471668 (ebook)
Subjects: LCSH: Rhinoceros beetle—Juvenile literature.
Classification: LCC QL596.S3 F56 2021 (print) | LCC QL596.S3 (ebook) |
  DDC 595.76/49—dc23
LC record available at https://lccn.loc.gov/2020008973
LC ebook record available at https://lccn.loc.gov/2020008974

For more information, write to Bearport Publishing, 5357 Penn Avenue South, Minneapolis, MN 55419. Printed in the United States of America.

Contents

AWESOME
Rhinoceros Beetles!

SLAM! A rhinoceros beetle uses its horns to throw another beetle off its branch. These horned battling beetles are awesome!

THE MALE RHINOCEROS
BEETLE HAS LARGE HORNS—
LIKE A RHINOCEROS!

Ready for Battle

There are about 300 kinds of rhinoceros beetles. While they are most well-known for their horns, that's not the only thing that makes these beetles ready for battle. Tough, bony armor covers their body. Even their wings are covered! A beetle's wings have two parts. The outer wings are hard. They protect the inner wings, which are thinner and used to fly.

Great Big Beetles

Rhinoceros beetles are usually black, gray, brown, or green. Some are shiny. Others have short, soft hair on their bodies. Some kinds of rhinoceros beetles grow up to 7 inches (17.8 cm) long!

Rhinoceros beetles are the strongest animals on Earth for their size. Some can lift about 850 times their own weight. That's like a person lifting nine elephants. **WOW!**

Hair

A Beetle Bodybuilder

Rhinoceros beetles are so strong that some kinds of these beetles are called Hercules beetles. In ancient Greek stories, Hercules was a hero known for his great strength.

That's not the only nickname these beetles have been given. They are also called elephant beetles, unicorn beetles, and Atlas beetles.

Home Sweet Home

Rhinoceros beetles live on every **continent** but Antarctica. Many rhinoceros beetles live in warm, wet places. They can be found on rain forest floors. Others live in woods under rotting logs where they can stay hidden and safe. They make their homes where there is plenty for them to eat.

RHINOCEROS BEETLES MIGHT HIDE IN PLAIN SIGHT. THEIR COLORING OFTEN KEEPS THEM **CAMOUFLAGED.**

What's on the Menu?

Rhinoceros beetles may look like scary **predators**. But don't worry. These big beetles only eat plants!

An adult beetle eats fresh and rotting fruit, **nectar**, and tree sap. The young rhinoceros beetle's diet is a little different. It includes dead trees and leaves. The beetle also munches on other rotting plants on the forest floor. **TASTY!**

RHINOCEROS BEETLES HELP BREAK DOWN DEAD PLANTS. THIS MAKES ROOM FOR OTHER PLANTS TO GROW.

A rhinoceros beetle eating a banana

Having a Hiss-y Fit

With their large size and fierce looks, rhinoceros beetles don't have many enemies. Their main predators are snakes and birds.

Luckily, rhinoceros beetles have some **defenses** they use to stay safe. They're active at night and hide during the day. A tough **exoskeleton** protects their bodies. And they make loud hissing sounds when disturbed!

A RHINOCEROS BEETLE DOESN'T *REALLY* HISS. IT MAKES SOUND BY RUBBING PARTS OF ITS WINGS AGAINST ITS BODY.

Battle of the Beetles

Although rhinoceros beetles don't have many predators, they do fight one another. Male beetles get into battles of big beetle horns!

CRASH! Male rhinoceros beetles lock horns. They fight over places to eat. They also fight over females. The female **mates** with the battle's winner. For her, the strongest male means strong beetle babies!

FEMALE RHINOCEROS BEETLES DON'T HAVE HORNS. THEY LEAVE THE FIGHTING TO THE MALES.

You Big Baby!

After mating, a female beetle lays about 50 eggs. In a few weeks, the eggs hatch into large, fat **grubs**. The hungry grubs eat a lot and grow even larger!

Rhinoceros beetles can stay grubs for a few years. They **molt** several times before becoming adults. Adult rhinoceros beetles mate, and the **cycle** starts all over again!

ADULT RHINOCEROS BEETLES LIVE FOR ONLY A FEW MONTHS.

A rhinoceros
beetle grub

RHINOCEROS BEETLES ARE AWESOME!
LET'S LEARN EVEN MORE ABOUT THEM.

Kind of animal: Rhinoceros beetles are insects. All insects have one or two sets of wings, six legs, and three body parts.

Other insects: Scientists think there are more than 900,000 different kinds of insects alive on Earth.

Size: Rhinoceros beetles can grow up to 7 in (17.8 cm) long. That's about the length of a new wooden pencil.

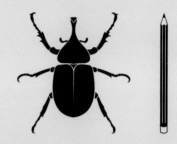

RHINOCEROS BEETLES AROUND THE WORLD

Arctic Ocean

NORTH AMERICA

EUROPE

ASIA

Pacific Ocean

Atlantic Ocean

AFRICA

Pacific Ocean

SOUTH AMERICA

Indian Ocean

AUSTRALIA

Southern Ocean

ANTARCTICA

N
W E
S

WHERE RHINOCEROS BEETLES LIVE

camouflaged blended in with the surroundings because of the colors and markings on a body

continent one of Earth's seven large land masses

cycle an order of events that happens over and over again

defenses the ways an animal keeps itself safe

exoskeleton an insect's hard outer covering

grubs insects at the wormlike stage of life

mates comes together with another to make babies

molt to shed an outer layer

nectar a sweet liquid made by plants

predators animals that hunt and kill other animals for food

Index

Read More

Chiger, Arielle. *20 Fun Facts About Beetles (Fun Fact File: Bugs!)*. New York: Gareth Stevens (2013).

Higgins, Melissa. *Brilliant Beetles: A 4D Book (Little Entomologist 4D)*. North Mankato, MN: Pebble (2019).

Polinsky, Paige V. *Rhinoceros Beetle: Heavyweight Champion (Animal Superstars)*. Minneapolis: Super Sandcastle (2017).

Learn More Online

1. Go to **www.factsurfer.com**
2. Enter "**Rhinoceros Beetle**" into the search box.
3. Click on the cover of this book to see a list of websites.

About the Author

Catherine C. Finan lives in northeastern Pennsylvania, where she often goes on nature hikes in search of awesome animals. One day she hopes to spot a rhinoceros beetle!